ENTREPRENEURSHIP: MONEY, WEALTH, & PROSPERITY

THE LONGEST WAY TO SUCCESS IS A SHORTCUT

Christopher Mitchell

www.ChangeYourLifeOvernight.com

ENTREPRENEURSHIP: MONEY, WEALTH, & PROSPERITY! THE LONGEST WAY TO SUCCESS IS A SHORTCUT.

Copyright © 2017 Christopher Mitchell

ISBN-13: 978-1545577486

ISBN-10: 154557748X

Unless otherwise noted, all scriptures quoted are from the New International Version (NIV) of The Holy Bible. Copyright 1973, 1978, 1984, 2011 by Biblica, Inc. Used by permission. All rights reserved worldwide.

All rights reserved. Under International Copyright Law no part of this publication may be reproduced, stored in a retrieval system or transmitted in any form- digital, electronic, mechanical, photocopy, recording or any other form without the prior written permission of the author or publisher.

Printed In The United States Of America.

TABLE OF CONTENTS:

1. Who Am I: 1
2. Numbers Don't Lie: 12
3. True Facts: 22
4. Your Reason Why: 32
5. Confession: 35
6. Attraction: 48
7. Hard Work & Sacrifice: 65
8. Commitment: 73
9. Take Action: 78
10. Don't Quit: 85
11. Dream Come True Business: 92

Christopher hopes this book will educate and inspire you to change your life financially forever. By implementing the information laid out in this book, you will absolutely create more money in your life. Money is good because you can't live without it. The more money you have access to means the more people you can be a blessing to. If you want to speak to Christopher, or perhaps join his team and have him become your personal mentor, feel free to contact him at his website. God bless you!

www.ChangeYourLifeOvernight.com

Chapter One:

Who Am I?

Who am I and why should you listen to me? My name is Christopher Paul Mitchell. I was born on January 9th, 1979, in Houston, Texas. Two years later my younger brother Andrew was born. My parents were complete opposites. My mom was an angel from Heaven. My dad, well, like I said, he was the opposite.

When I was three years old my dad cheated on my mom. My mom divorced my dad and became a single mother. She worked as a secretary at Ohio Wesleyan University in Delaware, Ohio. With a tiny salary, two young boys to feed, a car, apartment, insurance, as well as many other expenses to pay for, as you can probably imagine my mom struggled financially. I remember sitting on the living room floor when I was seven years old with my mom sitting behind me on the couch. I looked up at her and said these exact words that I will never forget for the rest of my life:

Mom, I'm going to be rich someday, and when that happens I'm going to take care of you and you're never going to struggle again. She looked me in the eyes, told me she believed me, and then started crying. Just two years later, when I was nine years old my mom suddenly died from cancer. It took everyone by surprise. She was perfectly healthy one day and then out of nowhere she was gone. She was only thirty-five years old.

It's been almost thirty years since my mom passed away, but I'm still holding on to life lessons that I learned from her. I was blessed to have the greatest mom in the world for nine years. She was the best! I'll never forget her. I look forward to the day when I get to see here again.

When my mom passed away my dad automatically regained custody of me and my brother. He had remarried and his wife had a daughter of her own. My dad also had a collection of cats and dogs that he couldn't properly care for. My brother and I were now living with my dad, his wife, her daughter, and a total of three cats and ten dogs.

It was a miserable living situation. My dad and his wife fought every single day without exception. My dad screamed every single time he opened his mouth. He was a terrible dad and a terrible husband. My brother and I stayed out of the house as much as we could because we feared being around our dad more than we feared The Devil. He was very hateful and abusive. All my mom did was love me and encourage me, while all my dad did was hate me and abuse me.

I joined the wrestling team and started working out when I became a freshman in high school. One day, after I arrived home from wrestling practice my dad was in one of his usual rages. He started yelling at me to clean the house and I simply said no! He didn't like that one bit, so he came toward me to beat me yet again, but this time something had changed. I had taken enough abuse from this man. I had gained a lot of size and strength from working out and something inside of me snapped! I had reached my breaking point! I defended myself against my dad.

Instead of him throwing me across the room, this time I picked him up and threw him across the room. After I threw him across the room I ran over to him, put him in a wrestling move, and completely popped both of his shoulders out of their sockets. His third wife at the time called 911 and the ambulance immediately rushed him to the emergency room. He stayed in the hospital for a few days because of the damage I had done to him physically. When he came home from the hospital he kicked me out of the house at that very moment.

I was only fifteen years old and unsure of where to go. I didn't even have my driver's license yet, let alone a car to get around in. I made some phone calls and ended up moving in with a few relatives. I moved in with my grandparents for a while, then I moved in with an Aunt for a while, and then I moved in with an Uncle for a while. I bounced around back and forth between these relatives houses until I became an official adult.

I received a government check for my mom's death when I turned eighteen years old. That check allowed me to buy my first car and move into my own apartment. I still had five months until I graduated high school, but I was already living on my own. At this point in my life I became a complete loner. I didn't hang out with people anymore. I was a health fanatic who ate healthy and took great care of my body, while all my so-called high school friends either drank beer or smoked pot every single day. I wasn't about to become another statistic who gave up on my goals and dreams in life just to become a loser. All I did was go to school, workout, and go to baseball practice. I hated school, but I had to attend in order to play baseball. Baseball was my life! I was good! Really good! My dream was to become a Major League Baseball Player. I had just one problem. I was small! Really small! That's why I started working out a few years earlier. I wanted to get bigger, faster, and stronger for baseball.

I went on to graduate high school just like everyone else, despite bouncing around for three years. I received a four year college scholarship for free from Ohio Wesleyan University in honor of my mom, but I knew college would never teach me how to become rich, so I told them to keep it. I passed on going to school and tried out for the big leagues instead. I went down to Lakeland, Florida to The Detroit Tigers spring training camp. I thought I was going to become rich by playing Major League Baseball, but I started having all kinds of pain in my joints. To make a long story short, I ended up having five surgeries in the next sixteen months on both of my elbows, both of my shoulders, and my right knee. I never played baseball again.

When I finally admitted to myself that I was never going to play baseball again, I got depressed. I moved to Los Angeles, California and got totally beat up by life. I got involved in everything. I started a personal training business. I became a fitness model. I became a male stripper. I even became a male prostitute. I was so unhappy at one point that I drove to Malibu and almost committed suicide by jumping off a high cliff over-looking the ocean.

I've moved over one hundred times throughout my lifetime. I've lived in nine different states and I've been homeless in five of them. I've started over twenty-five businesses and failed in every single one of them.

I've been in a car crash where the paramedics had to cut my car to pieces with the jaws of life to get me out. I caught the woman who I was about to marry cheating on me. I've been evicted from apartments, I've had my cars repossessed, I've had my bank accounts overdrawn so many times I can't even keep track, and I've even had a jealous hater falsely accuse me of being a scam artist, a child rapist, a gay porn star, and a dangerous threat to society. He said all of this while he was under oath in a court room. It couldn't have been further from the truth. Everything he said was a downright lie.

I just shared a brief history of my life with you so you can see where I came from, see what I've been through, and see that I'm a normal person who has lived a life of chaos just like most people. However, unlike most people, I didn't quit. I never gave up despite all the hell I went through.

Like 98% of the world's population, I was dead broke for the first part of my life. That's why you should listen to me when it comes to money, wealth, and prosperity. I came from the bottom just like most people. I failed so many times that I stopped keeping track years ago. I was so broke most of my life that I couldn't even pay attention. However, I stayed the course, refused to quit, and learned some valuable skills that turned my life around. I'm now an international best-selling author and successful business owner.

I'm one of the absolute best people you could ever learn from when it comes to entrepreneurship because I've failed so many times. I can teach you two important things that will save you a lot of time, money, and heartache. These two things are:

1. What to do.

2. What not to do.

In this book, I'm going to teach you everything I've learned throughout my lifetime about money, wealth, and prosperity so you can become a successful entrepreneur ten times faster than it took me to. If you'll take the information I give you in this book and start implementing it, I promise that success will come to you in every area of your life. If you're ready to say goodbye to poverty and say hello to money, wealth, and prosperity, then let's get started!

Chapter Two:

Numbers Don't Lie!

Did you know that 98% of America's population is dead broke?

Did you know that 98% of America's population are employees?

Did you know that only 2% of America's population is wealthy?

Did you know that only 2% of America's population are business owners?

Based on these numbers, it doesn't take a genius to figure out if you want to be wealthy in life you must be a business owner. I'm pretty sure the 98% know this, but I'm not sure why they continue to be employees. You see, numbers don't lie. Whether you're male or female, young or old, black or white, live in America or

Saudi Arabia, two plus two equals four everywhere in the world, every single day of the week. Why you ask? Because numbers don't lie. I'm going to spend some time in this chapter talking about numbers for that very reason. Once you understand the power of numbers it will teach you how to generate money, wealth, and prosperity a lot faster. Pay close attention! Let me remind you what the title of this book is:

ENTREPRENEURSHIP: MONEY, WEALTH, & PROSPERITY!

While the subtitle of this book is:
THE LONGEST WAY TO SUCCESS IS A SHORTCUT.

Again, I wanted to bring this to your attention for the simple fact that if you want to experience more money, wealth, and prosperity in your life, you must become a business owner, if you're not already. Not only do you have to be a business owner, but you must never take shortcuts. Trying to take a shortcut on your way to success will postpone it even longer. This book will definitely teach you about entrepreneurship, but you must be willing to act on what you learn. No one ever became successful by simply reading a book, but many people became successful doing what they learned from reading a book.

An entrepreneur is someone who will get downright sick to their stomach even thinking about what it would be like to work for someone else as an employee. Entrepreneurs are the people who make up the 2% class. For the most part, entrepreneurs are "C" students in school. They're the ones who create companies and have the "A" students work for them.

Entrepreneurs are the few people who control all the money, wealth, and prosperity in the world. They should though. Entrepreneurs are risk takers. They live their lives by faith, while everyone else lives by sight. That's why they make more money. They're willing to do things when everyone else is scared. If the world didn't have entrepreneurs the world wouldn't exist. There's so much more money for entrepreneurs than for employees because the competition is so much smaller.

You must remember that 98% of America's population are employees. That's a lot of people fighting for just a few jobs. However, only 2% of America's population are writing their own paychecks as entrepreneurs. Don't you think you would pay yourself more than your boss does? Then do it!

To become an entrepreneur, you must first stop making the excuses you've made up to this point as to why you haven't been one yet. As of right now, if you're not currently a business owner it's only because of one or more of the following excuses:

-I'm too old.

-I'm too young.

-I'm married with kids.

-I don't have the time.

-I don't have the skills.

-I don't have the money.

Well, guess what? You can make money, or you can make excuses, but you can't make both. So, you're going to have to choose right now which one it's going to be? Entrepreneurs make a lot of money because they don't make any excuses.

After you read the following numbers you no longer have a right to make excuses. If you want to have a lot of money, wealth, and prosperity, you have to release all of your excuses.

Did you know that forty years old is the average age of people who start their own business?

Did you know that less than 1% of business owners came from extremely rich backgrounds?

Did you know that 70% of business owners were married when they started their first business?

Did you know that 60% of business owners had at least one child when they started their first business?

Did you know that 75% of business owners worked as employees for at least six years before they started their first business?

So, based on these facts, it doesn't matter what your age is, what your background is, whether you're married with kids, or whether you've been working as an employee your entire life up to this point. The only thing that matters is that you stop making excuses and start your own business right now.

Did you know that only 2% of the population in the United States is made up of entrepreneurs?

This should get you excited! This is awesome news! This just goes to show you how unlimited the opportunities are in America. Only 2% of the entire country are entrepreneurs. Everyone else is fighting for a dead end job. No wonder the unemployment rate is so high. There's too many people and not enough jobs. That means there's more money, wealth, and prosperity for the entrepreneurs, which is exactly why the rich keep getting richer and the poor keep getting poorer. Entrepreneurship is simply a choice. Those who choose to be entrepreneurs choose to be rich, while those who choose to be employees choose to be poor. What makes a person have a lot of money, wealth, and prosperity is nothing more than a choice!

Now that you know money, wealth, prosperity, and entrepreneurship are all choices, don't you think it's time for you to start making different choices? When do you think would be the best time for you to change your life? Now or later? Alright then, what are you waiting for? Become an entrepreneur right now! Here's five great reasons why you should start your own business immediately:

1. Money! Being an entrepreneur can make you a lot of money. A lot more money than you would ever be able to make as an employee.

2. Freedom! Being an entrepreneur allows you to be your own boss, call your own shots, and not have anyone tell you what to do anymore.

3. Control! Being an entrepreneur gives you control over your time and money. You decide how much time you want to work and how much money you want to make.

4. Choices! Being an entrepreneur gives you choices. You choose who you work with every day. You choose when to take a lunch break. You choose when you go on vacation.

5. Legacy! Being an entrepreneur gives you the opportunity to leave a legacy behind for your heirs.

I hope you see how amazing life can be as an entrepreneur? In my opinion, there's really no other way to live. Being an employee is the same thing as being a slave. I'll never understand why someone would voluntarily put themselves through that for fifty years. Every employee I've ever known hates their job, feels like they're overworked, feels like they're underpaid, and wastes their entire life doing something they don't enjoy. Life is too short for that! Stop making excuses and start taking action! It's time for you to become an entrepreneur right now!

Chapter Three:

True Facts.

So, you say you want to be an entrepreneur? Time will tell because talk is cheap. Actions speak louder than words. I never listen to what people say, I watch what they do. I want to give you some facts about entrepreneurship, not to discourage you, but to see if you have what it takes. To see if you're going to follow through on what you say you're going to do. To see if you're going to keep pressing on when times get tough.

People are sick and tired of working at a dead end job for someone else only to get a paycheck that doesn't even cover their monthly living expenses. More and more people are taking a leap of faith by starting their own businesses than ever before.

However, entrepreneurship isn't easy. Most people think the thought of owning a business sounds great, but they're not prepared mentally to overcome obstacles. As soon as they experience any kind of setback, they immediately throw in the towel and go back to working for The Devil. Ooops, I mean corporate America.

The majority of people in the world simply think that owning their own business is a quick way to a lot of money, wealth, and prosperity. However, the longest way to success is a shortcut. People think that by cutting corners or skipping out on doing research will get them to success faster, but the very opposite is true. Less than 2% of the world's population are rich and successful. This is only because very few people are willing to put in the work and sacrifice that is required. Most people have a lazy, lottery mentality and when they don't get rich in a week they give up. These types of people don't have what it takes to be entrepreneurs. Here's some facts to prepare you for the road ahead:

-One in about every twenty people worldwide consider themselves to be an entrepreneur.

-The average employee works forty hours per week, but the average entrepreneur works more than sixty hours per week.

-The average employee only makes $28,000 per year, but the average entrepreneur makes $55,000 per year.

-The United States has the top economy in the world, but only 2% of the population are entrepreneurs.

-The average investment is $30,000 to start your own business.

Based on the facts just listed, being an entrepreneur will require you to work more hours than a typical employee. I believe this is why very few people are entrepreneurs because most people don't want to work very hard. Most people in the world today are downright lazy, especially the people in America. However, if you're willing to put in some time and hard work, I'll introduce you to a business model you can start in your home:

-That will cost you less than $1,000 to get started, instead of $30,000.

-That can make you millions of dollars, instead of only $55,000.

I'll talk to you more about this in a later chapter, but for now, let's continue. Another fact about being an entrepreneur is that you will save a fortune on your taxes.

The United States Government loves entrepreneurs because of what they do for the economy. This love from the government rewards people who are entrepreneurs with a big savings when it comes time to pay taxes. I always tell people that it doesn't matter how much money you make, but how much money you keep. An entrepreneur will always have more money than an employee because the government gives them tax deductions. Most broke employees complain about rich entrepreneurs paying less in taxes than they do, but what they should be doing is starting their own business, so they too can pay less in taxes. Instead of being jealous of the rich, I encourage you to join them instead.

Just in case you don't know what a tax deduction is, let me explain that to you first:

Tax deduction: something that helps you save money on your taxes at the end of the year. A tax deduction has a cash value when it comes time to file your taxes.

In America, we pay taxes on what is called the Adjusted Gross Income. This is the money you make minus the deductions you legally qualify for. Let's use Bob as an example. Bob earns $50,000 per year at his current job. As an employee, he would pay taxes on all $50,000 of his income.

Now, in the next example, Bob is an entrepreneur and owns a home-based business. Let's say Bob also earns $50,000 per year as a business owner, but he qualifies for $10,000 in tax deductions. This means that Bob would only have to pay taxes on $40,000 instead of $50,000 like he did when he was an employee because he gets to deduct $10,000 from his income for expenses.

If Bob is in the 25% tax bracket, then this means he saved $2,500 in taxes. Not bad huh? I don't know about you, but an extra $2,500 that stays in my pocket is much better than if I had to give it to the government. As they say, a penny saved is a penny earned. Getting rich isn't just about how much money you make. It's all about how much money you keep. Being an entrepreneur by having your own home-based business allows you to keep a lot more of your money because of tax write offs, instead of giving it away to the government. That reason alone should be why every single person in the world starts their own business.

Let me break this down for you a little bit more in detail. I'll continue to use Bob as the example. Bob made $50,000 last year at his job. He was happy during tax season because he received a $1,500 tax refund. However, he's not going to be happy when he finds out what I'm going to say next. You see, Bob had already paid out around $11,500 to the IRS from the money that was taken out from each of his paychecks.

So therefore, he actually paid $10,000 in taxes. What if Bob could get back more at the end of the year? What if he could get back closer to $10,000? I'm going to show you how this would have been possible for Bob if he was an entrepreneur with his own home-based business. Allow me to introduce you to the powerful savings of tax deductions.

Let's look at Bob's monthly expenses:
Car costs.
Eating out.
Cell phone bill.
Gas & electricity.
Mortgage payment.

As an employee, Bob doesn't get any tax deductions from these expenses. However, as a home-based business owner a portion of these expenses would be tax deductible. Let's say that Bob's cell phone bill is $100 per month. That's a total of $1,200 per year in expenses.

Since Bob is in the 25% tax bracket this means he would save $300 at the end of the year just from his cell phone bill alone. You get this number by taking $1,200 and multiplying it by 25%. He's spending the same amount of money on his cell phone bill each year that the rest of his coworkers spent when he was an employee. However, since he now owns a home-based business, he actually gets to save $300 more every year than he did when he was an employee. That's how the rich get richer and the poor get poorer. The rich pay less in taxes. In order to pay less in taxes, you must get some tax deductions from the government. The best way to do this is to own a home-based business.

Chapter Four:

Your Reason Why.

Why do you want to become an entrepreneur? You must be able to answer this question with laser beam accuracy, otherwise you'll give up on your goals and dreams as soon as the first obstacle comes your way. Your reason "why" needs to be so big that it makes you cry. You can't say you want to become an entrepreneur just because you want more money. You can't say you want to become an entrepreneur just because you don't like working at your current job. You can't say you want to become an entrepreneur just because you want to be your own boss. These things have no real meaning to you. Your reason "why" needs to come from the bottom of your heart. It needs to get you out of bed in the morning.

Your reason "why" needs to be the motivation behind every single thing that you do. When obstacles try to destroy you, your reason "why" will keep you going. When all your current friends and family members are getting together for happy hour your reason "why" will give you the strength to tell them that you won't be there. When your bank account is overdrawn because your business isn't turning a profit yet your reason "why" will remind you to stay positive. Your reason "why" will be the only thing that keeps you going when everything in the world is coming against you.

When I was seven years old, I made a promise to my mom that I was going to become rich someday and take care of her. My mom died two years later, but she has been my reason "why" for over thirty years. I have never made a promise to someone that I didn't keep, especially to the most important person in the world to me, which was my mom. On August 28th, 2014, I married my soulmate Stacy. She is identical to my mom. So, she has now become my reason "why" along with my mom.

Besides my father in Heaven, my wife and my mom will always be the most important people in the world to me. They are the strongest reason "why" that I could ever have. No matter what life might bring against me, I will never quit on these two amazing women. I would die for them and kill for them. I would do anything for them. Your reason "why" needs to be as strong as mine. Once your reason "why" is that strong, absolutely nothing in the entire world will be able to stop you from achieving your goals and dreams in life. Nothing!

Chapter Five:

Confession.

The Law Of Confession states that the words you speak will manifest in your life because words are seeds. If you want to become an entrepreneur with an abundant supply of money, wealth, and prosperity, you absolutely must use the law of confession to your advantage. In order for you to succeed in life you have to start speaking positive affirmations over yourself and your business every single day of your life. The most powerful words that you could ever speak over yourself are scriptures from the Holy Bible. I'm going to show you how important it is to speak empowering words over yourself and your business. Let me share some scriptures with you to prove how powerful words are.

Believing and speaking the word of God is a very powerful law that can truly change your life. God created the entire universe simply by speaking words. See for yourself:

God said, let there be light and there was light. **Genesis 1:3**

God said, let there be a vault between the waters to separate water from water. **Genesis 1:6**

God said, let the water under the sky be gathered to one place and let dry ground appear. **Genesis 1:9**

God said, let the land produce vegetation; seed bearing plants and trees on the land that bear fruit with seed in it according to their various kinds. **Genesis 1:11**

God said, let there be lights in the vault of the sky to separate the day from the night, and let them serve as signs to mark sacred times, days and years, and let them be lights in the vault of the sky to give light on the earth. **Genesis 1:14-15**

God said, let the water teem with living creatures and let birds fly above the earth across the vault of the sky. **Genesis 1:20**

God said, let the land produce living creatures according to their kinds: the livestock, the creatures that move along the ground, and the wild animals each according to its kind. **Genesis 1:24**

God said, let us make mankind in our image, in our likeness, so that they may rule over the fish in the sea and the birds in the sky, over the livestock and all the wild animals, and over all the creatures that move along the ground. **Genesis 1:26**

This is amazing! Not only did God create the entire universe simply by speaking it into existence, but he created you in his image and likeness. That means he gave you the same exact power and authority with the words that you speak. Your words have amazing power. Your words can literally change any circumstance in your life. That's why it's extremely important to only speak about things that you want. Never speak about things that you don't want. The words that you speak will absolutely manifest in your life.

Growing up as children, we always heard the saying: sticks and stones will break my bones, but words will never hurt me. As adults, we know the complete opposite is true. Sticks and stones have never broken any bones, but hurtful words have been known to cause all kinds of illness, sickness, and disease. Some people have committed suicide because of the power of hurtful words.

Children who have parents that speak negatively to them all the time grow up with inferiority complexes. If you're a parent make sure you only speak positive words to your children. Encourage them with your words. Remind them with your words that they're blessed and that they can achieve anything they set their mind to. Build them up with your words instead of tearing them down.

Do you ever notice that poor people always say things like:

~I can't afford that.

~Money is the root of all evil.

~Money doesn't grow on trees.

~I'd rather be happy than be rich.

Every time a person speaks negative words about money like that they're only cursing themselves financially. They're setting themselves up to be poor forever. If you say you can't afford something you're absolutely right. You'll never be able to afford it.

Instead of confessing how poor you are all the time, start confessing how rich you are. Jesus came to give us life and give it to us in abundance. Abundance is having a lot of money, wealth, and prosperity. Abundance is having so much you can't count it. Start confessing what the Holy Bible says about your finances instead of what your bank statements say about your finances. Confessing God's word over your finances will change what your bank statements say. Stop trying to figure out how your circumstances are going to change and just start believing in what God's word says.

You don't have to know how. All you need to know is that speaking God's word will change any situation in the natural world if you'll simply believe what you speak. That's how the law of confession works. You have to believe and then speak the word of God! Let's see what the Holy Bible says about being able to change your circumstances just by confessing scriptures over them.

The blessing of the Lord brings me wealth without painful toil for it. **Proverbs 10:22**

The tongue has the power of life and death, and those who love it will eat its fruit. **Proverbs 18:21**

My word that goes out from my mouth will not return to me empty, but will accomplish what I desire and achieve the purpose for which I sent it. **Isaiah 55:11**

By your words you will be acquitted, and by your words you will be condemned. **Matthew 12:37**

If I say to this mountain, go throw yourself into the sea, and do not doubt in my heart, but believe what I say will happen, it will be done for me. **Mark 11:23**

I give life to the dead and call into being things that were not.
Romans 4:17

Do not let any unwholesome talk come out of your mouth, but only what is helpful for building others up according to their needs, that it may benefit those who listen.
Ephesians 4:29

I remember telling people when I was seventeen years old that I was going to become a professional fitness model and appear on the covers of fitness magazines all over the world. Every single person laughed at me and told me I was crazy. However, I kept confessing over and over to myself every single day that I would appear on the covers of fitness magazines. A year later, when I was eighteen years old, I appeared on my first magazine cover. I had spoken that into existence just like God spoke the universe into existence.

If you have a car loan, a mortgage loan, or credit card loans, that means you're in debt! Use The Law Of Confession to get yourself out of debt. Take your car loan, your mortgage loan, and your credit card loans and speak to them. Listen up car loan, I command that you be completely paid off in the name of Jesus! Listen up mortgage loan, I command that you be completely paid off in the name of Jesus! Listen up credit card loans, I command that you be completely paid off in the name of Jesus!

Use The Law Of Confession to bring in more money. Open up your empty purse or wallet and speak to it. Listen up purse, I decree and declare that you are now filled with hundred dollar bills. I command that money comes to me right now! Every single day I receive money from the north, south, east, and west.

Use The Law Of Confession to reprogram your poverty mindset into a prosperous mindset. Look yourself in the mirror every single day and repeat out loud: I am rich! Money, wealth, and prosperity are mine! I am successful! I am a Multi-Millionaire! Money comes to me easily and abundantly every single day! My sales are increasing right now! New opportunities come to me every single day! I am rich in every way so that I can be generous on every occasion.

Don't think you're too good to look at yourself in the mirror and talk to yourself like this. Look at the power of what your words can do. Your words can absolutely eliminate your debt and bring in huge sums of money supernaturally from places you can't even imagine. But, you have to confess the word of God!

Jesus knew how powerful his words are. He killed a fig tree with his words. Look at this set of scriptures:

The next day as they were leaving Bethany, Jesus was hungry. Seeing in the distance a fig tree in leaf, he went to find out if it had any fruit. When he reached it he found nothing but leaves because it was not the season for figs. Then he said to the tree, may no one ever eat fruit from you again. And his disciples heard him say it. **Mark 11:12-14**

Believe it, then speak it! Your words can change your entire life. The power of your words is beyond comprehending. Confessing the word of God over your life will change any circumstance you might be dealing with. There is nothing in the entire world that cannot be turned around by the power of your words. Most people in the world today don't understand the connection between the words they speak and the life they live. Jesus explains how powerful words are in this verse:

The Spirit gives life, the flesh counts for nothing. The words I have spoken to you, they are full of the Spirit and life. **John 6:63**

If any area of your life needs turned around, simply speak the word of God over it. If you want to become a successful entrepreneur with an abundant supply of money, wealth, and prosperity, start tapping into this ancient Biblical secret and watch your life transform in every area.

Law: If you want to have an abundant supply of money, wealth, and prosperity, you must only confess what you want in life. Never confess what you don't want.

Chapter Six:

Attraction.

The Law Of Attraction states that whatever you focus on you're going to attract into your life because thoughts are things.

The Law Of Attraction could also be called visualization. What are you constantly visualizing on a regular basis? Do you visualize getting bills in the mail every single day, or do you visualize getting paychecks in the mail every single day? You know what the answer is based on what you're getting in the mail every single day.

Have you ever visualized yourself getting caught in a traffic jam? If so, what happened? You got caught in a traffic jam didn't you? Have you ever visualized yourself arriving late to work in the morning? If so, what happened? You arrived late to work didn't you? Have you ever visualized yourself running into an old friend you haven't seen in a long time? If so, what happened? You ran into them didn't you? This is the powerful Law Of Attraction at work in your life. I can always look back to the past and figure out what I was focusing on during that period of time based on what I was attracting into my life.

I remember seeing a beautiful girl with blonde hair sitting in the bleachers when I was sixteen years old playing in one of my baseball games. I stared at her when I walked up to the plate when it was my turn to bat. I stared at her when I was in the field playing shortstop. I stared at her when I ran off the field to the dugout when the innings were over. I had never seen her before, but I couldn't get her out of my mind. I didn't know her name. I didn't know who she was. I didn't even know who she was cheering for. All I knew is that I wanted to meet her, talk to her, and go out on a date with her. By the time the game was over and I packed up my equipment she was gone. She was nowhere to be seen. I thought about her later that night. I thought about her while I was in school. I thought about her when I was at baseball practice. I thought about her all the time.

About a month later I received a phone call from a girl I didn't know. I asked her who she was since I didn't recognize her voice. She said, I'm the blonde girl that was sitting in the bleachers watching your baseball game about a month ago. What? I yelled in excitement! Are you kidding me? How in the world did you get my phone number? How did you find out who I was? What are you calling me for? She said, I thought you were cute. I wanted to talk to you after your game, but I had to leave. So, I started asking around. Sure enough, I tracked you down. That's amazing I said! I'm so glad you did. I haven't stopped thinking about you since that day. We started dating at that very moment. That was the powerful Law Of Attraction at work in my life.

That story clearly shows you how powerful our thoughts are. I focused on her for an entire month. She didn't even go to my school, but my laser beam, focused thoughts attracted her into my life. What I focused on, also known as The Law Of Attraction, worked for me.

As a little boy growing up, I loved the Rocky movies played by Sylvester Stallone. I must have watched those movies at least a hundred times. I knew every single word in every movie. I visualized myself being Rocky in the movies. I would punch the same way that he punched. I would talk the same way that he talked. I would even mimic every move that he made. I focused on playing the role of Rocky by Sylvester Stallone so much that he started to dominate my thoughts. I wanted to meet him so badly. I wanted to tell him how much I loved watching his movies.

Well, years later when I was in my twenties, I worked as a vendor at a supplement booth in Columbus, Ohio at the annual Arnold Schwarzenegger Bodybuilding Expo. While walking through thousands of people to get to my booth I suddenly came across a huge mob of people blocking all the walk ways. I was surrounded by people and there was nowhere to go.

I asked some people crammed up next to me what was going on? They said, Sylvester Stallone is about fifty yards ahead.

OMG! I couldn't believe it. The man I idolized growing up as a little boy was now fifty yards in front me? Are you serious? I knew this was my moment. I knew this was my chance, but how would I ever meet him when he's surrounded by security guards and thousands of fans? I didn't know the answer, but I did know without a doubt in my mind that I was going to meet him that day. I remembered this amazing story in the Holy Bible:

In **Luke 8:43-48**, the Holy Bible talks about the woman who had the issue of blood. She wanted her healing. She visualized her healing. She knew that if she could just reach out and touch Jesus she would be healed. However, she had a problem. Jesus was in the middle of thousands of people. That didn't matter to her though. She was determined to make her way through those thousands of people no matter what she had to do. Nothing was going to stop her from getting her healing.

Sure enough, she put The Law Of Attraction to work. She didn't focus on what she didn't want, which was having to get through thousands of people. She only focused on what she did want, which was touching Jesus, so she could be healed. She got her healing. What she focused on, also known as The Law Of Attraction, worked for her.

My situation was similar. I focused on getting to Sylvester Stallone that day as much as that woman focused on getting to Jesus. I was determined.

Nothing was going to stop me. What I focused on, also known as The Law Of Attraction, worked for me. I got to meet and take my picture with Sylvester Stallone that day. One of my favorite scriptures that I live by every single day is:

Do not conform to the pattern of this world, but be transformed by the renewing of your mind. **Romans 12:2**

This verse tells us not to think the way the rest of the world thinks. The rest of the world would have just given up in these situations. They would have focused on the obstacle, not on the prize. You can have whatever you want in your life if you'll just believe that you can. Focus on what you want, visualize what you want, and believe that it is already yours. See yourself driving your dream car, living in your dream home, and living out all your goals and dreams in life. The Law Of Attraction states that whatever you focus on you're going to attract into your life because thoughts are things.

I was living in Chicago, Illinois back in 2007. While driving to an event my tires ran over some black ice and in a matter of seconds my life would change for the worse. I woke up to the sounds of sirens and the jaws of life cutting my car to pieces to get me and the passenger out of my car. My car was demolished. By the grace of God we lived. It took a while to recover, but today we're both fine.

I healed physically and started renewing my mind to the word of God. I was offered a six-figure position as a personal trainer with a company in Florida. However, I had a few problems. I didn't have a car, I didn't have any money, and I didn't have good credit. So, how in the world would I be able to get a new car so that I could drive back and forth to my job once I arrived in Florida?

I remembered The Law Of Attraction. I knew that it looked impossible for me to get a new car in the natural, but I also knew that what I focus on I get. So, instead of focusing on not having any money, or good credit, I only focused on getting a new car.

At this point in my life I didn't have the prosperous mindset that I have today. So, instead of focusing on a Lamborghini, I just focused on a lesser priced car. I walked to the Honda dealership in downtown Chicago. I found a brand new, sparkling, red, 2008 Honda Civic sitting on the showroom floor. That's the car I wanted. I accepted it by faith right then and there. A car salesman walked up to me and I told him this was the car I wanted. He told me to follow him back to his desk. He asked me if I had good credit for financing and I told him no I didn't. He then asked me, how do you think you're going to get a brand new car with bad credit? I told him I didn't know how, but I knew that my God would deliver it. He rolled his eyes at me.

He had me fill out a credit application hoping that I might get approved anyway. After he ran my credit, he realized I was telling him the truth. He told me there was no way I was going to be able to get that car. I smiled, and told him with God ALL things are possible! I then left the dealership. As I walked away I started visualizing myself sitting in the car, driving the car, and enjoying the car in the Florida sun. This intense focusing is a very real process. When you focus on something with great intensity it makes it feel like you already have the thing that you're focusing on.

I bought a plane ticket from Chicago to Orlando with every last penny that I had. I would arrive in Orlando on Friday and start working at my new job on Monday morning. In my spirit, I just knew, that I knew, that I knew, that somehow, someway, I was going to get that brand new Honda Civic. I just didn't know how. That's ok though. I just kept believing in The Law Of Attraction and focused on having the car in my possession. I would leave the rest up to God.

On Friday morning, just hours before I would fly to Orlando, I received this email from a complete stranger:

Hi Christopher, you don't know me, but I met you a few years ago in Columbus, Ohio at the Arnold Schwarzenegger Bodybuilding Expo. I got a copy of the bodybuilding magazine you were on the cover of that month and you autographed it for me. I only talked to you for a few minutes because other people were waiting in line to meet you. However, you were the nicest bodybuilder I had ever met. I just wanted to say it was a pleasure to meet you. If you ever need anything, please feel free to contact me anytime. Sincerely, Bill.

That was the exact email that I received from Bill. The thing that jumped out of his email the most was: If you ever need anything please feel free to contact me anytime. I thought to myself, well, I need a car. So, I decided to email him back and tell him what happened.

I told him I was in a bad car crash. I told him I just got offered a six-figure position as a personal trainer in Florida, but I didn't have a car to get back and forth. I asked him if he was a Christian and if he was to please pray for me that God would somehow bring me a car. That's all I said to him in my email. He emailed me back within one hour and here's what he said:

Christopher, I'm so sorry to hear about what happened to you. I know you don't know me, but I'm the CEO of a bank. I have perfect credit and plenty of money. You left such an impression on me when I met you that I would be thrilled to buy you a car. Please call me! Sincerely, Bill.

To make a long story short, he told me to go to the Honda dealership once I arrived in Orlando. When I picked out the car that I wanted, call him, and put him on the phone with the salesman. He would take care of the rest. I went to the Honda dealership as soon as I arrived in Orlando. I found the same exact, brand new, sparkling, red, 2008 Honda Civic sitting on the showroom floor that I saw in the Chicago showroom.

I called Bill, put him on the phone with the car salesman, and two hours later I drove off the car lot with a brand new car without paying a penny for it. It was unbelievable! I drove into an empty parking lot and started to cry. I couldn't believe the way God had come through for me. He used a complete stranger to buy me a brand new car. I think I would have had better odds winning the lottery than have that happening to me, but it did. God is truly amazing!

I had my part to play though and that's where most people miss it. I had to focus on what I wanted, confess it with my mouth, and receive it by faith! Then, just sit back, relax, and trust in God to bring it to me, which he did in the most unbelievable way a person could ever imagine. What I focused on, also known as The Law Of Attraction, worked for me.

Here's a visualization method you can use to focus on what you want in life. Lay down on your back in a quiet place with no distractions. Imagine yourself laying on the shore of the ocean. Your feet are closest to the water. Inhale deep breaths. As you breathe in imagine the waves are coming in toward you. As you breathe out imagine the waves going back out to sea. With every breath you take calm those waves down until the water is completely still. Now your breathing should be very relaxed. This is a deep meditative state that you're in. Now, begin to visualize the life you want. See yourself driving your dream car, living in your huge mansion, having the perfect physical body, traveling the world to all your favorite places, giving millions of dollars away to the needy, and even being healed from cancer. Whatever it is that you desire in life, visualize it, and make it real right now! The more you focus on the life you want the faster it will manifest in your physical world.

Law: If you want to have an abundant supply of money, wealth, and prosperity, you must only focus on what you want. Don't ever focus on what you don't want.

Chapter Seven:

Hard Work & Sacrifice.

Hard work and sacrifice? Are you kidding me? Are you really going to waste my time by making me read an entire chapter about hard work and sacrifice? Duh, everyone knows you need to work hard and sacrifice. Now, hopefully you didn't just speak that out loud, but I imagine some people will, which is why I started the chapter off that way.

Obviously, yes, I wrote a chapter about hard work and sacrifice, and for good reason as I'm about to point out. It doesn't matter what you know, it only matters what you do. Remember that! If everyone knows you need to work hard and sacrifice, then why do only 2% do it? Like I just mentioned, it doesn't matter that you know you need to work hard and sacrifice, it only matters that you do it. I want to remind you what I said back in chapter three about work ethic. The average employee works only forty hours per week, but the average entrepreneur works more than sixty hours per week. So, it's quite obvious that most people do not work hard or sacrifice, even if they know they should.

In America, most five year old boys start playing tee ball. By the time these boys get to ten years old some of them have already stopped playing. When these boys become freshman in high school at the age of fifteen a big percentage of them are no longer playing baseball. They start smoking and drinking to impress the upper classmen. By the time these boys reach the age of eighteen less than 1% of them are still playing.

What happened to all these boys? If you asked every single boy when they were five years old if they had a dream of becoming a Major League Baseball Player every single one of them would have told you yes. If this is the case, then why do so few of them go on to play baseball in the big leagues? I'll tell you why: hard work and sacrifice!

Every year from tee ball onward requires a boy to work harder and sacrifice more. Every year that a boy stays in baseball requires him to get bigger, faster, and stronger to remain competitive. In order to do this, he must work harder and sacrifice more. Well, most people aren't willing to do that. This is why most people will never become successful in anything in life. Instead of working hard and making sacrifices they would rather be lazy and insignificant.

However, this isn't just the case for boys in baseball. This is the case for both boys and girls in absolutely everything in life. This includes every sport, every extra-curricular activity, every musical instrument, even every single hobby. Let me prove it!

Most people love hearing the sound of a beautiful piano, but a great pianist is hard to find. If one million people started playing the piano when they were just three years old, how many of them do you think would go on to make a living from playing the piano as an adult? If you said less than 1% you're correct. The average four to six year old who plays the piano in America plays for three hours every single day. In China, they play for six hours every single day. For the very few who are still playing piano at the age of eighteen, they are now playing for eight hours every single day. That's a total of fifty-six hours every single week. That equates to more than nine full days of actual piano time every single month. Nine full days! Most people aren't willing to do this. However, the one in a million who is willing to pay this ultimate price is rewarded with millions of dollars in income. The world will pay a lot of money for excellence, but only a select few are willing to put in this kind of hard work and sacrifice to achieve this kind of a reward. The bigger the dream that you have, means the bigger the price you have to pay.

Entrepreneurship is no different. Everyone in the entire world knows that business owners make more money than employees do, but yet, only 2% of these people own their own business. Why is that? Because 98% of America's population aren't willing to work hard or make sacrifices. They're lazy! They want to get rich without doing anything. They have a lottery mentality. They simply want to pay a dollar and win three hundred million dollars in return.

Americans spent seventy billion dollars on lottery games in 2014. That's more than three hundred dollars per adult in the forty-three states where lotteries are legal. In fact, Americans spent more money on lottery tickets that year than they did on books, movie tickets, sporting events, video games, and recorded music combined. That's insane!

The odds of winning the Powerball jackpot are one in two hundred ninety-two million. Why would you waste your money on something with such a small chance like that? The average person in America who plays the lottery will lose $0.40 for every $1.00 in tickets that they buy. That's a terrible return on investment. That is definitely not the business strategy you want to partake in if having a lot of money, wealth, and prosperity is your goal. That's a guaranteed recipe for going bankrupt, which explains why 98% of the population is dead broke. This is their mindset and game plan for getting rich. Getting a dead end job at McDonald's would be a better wealth strategy than trying to win the lottery.

I can teach you how to become an entrepreneur and start a home-based business for less than $1,000. That's it! I know, because that's what I did and that's where all my money comes from. However, you're going to have to work hard, make some sacrifices, and learn some new skills, but the return on your investment could possibly be millions of dollars. I personally do not know of a better business model anywhere in the world. That's why I'm so passionate about sharing what I know with others. It has changed my family's lives forever and we have only just begun. Our future is limitless!

I'm going to tell you about my personal business model, but I want you to know ahead of time that you must be willing to work hard, make sacrifices, and learn some new skills. If you're willing to do these three things, then you'll be able to create the lifestyle of your dreams. If you truly want to have a life of unlimited money, wealth, and prosperity, keep reading.

Chapter Eight:
Commitment.

Commitment means doing what you said you would do long after the mood you said it in has left you. I love this definition. Oh, but how rare is the individual who actually does this. For 98% of the population to be dead broke means that they were unwilling to make a commitment to getting rich. For 50% of all first marriages to end in divorce means that one or both people were unwilling to make a commitment of staying together forever. For 66% of students to drop out of college means that they were unwilling to make a commitment of sticking it out until they graduated with a degree. For 70% of the population to be obese or overweight means that they were unwilling to make a commitment to losing weight and becoming healthy. A person who is willing to make a commitment to anything in life nowadays is very rare indeed.

In February of 1996, I started bodybuilding. I made a lifetime commitment to eating healthy, exercising on a regular basis, and taking nutritional supplements to help me live a long, healthy lifestyle. It has now been twenty-two years and I have stayed true to my commitment. I have maintained an organic diet, worked out regularly, and taken only the best protein shakes and supplements that money can buy. The result? I have perfect health and vitality, I haven't been to a Doctor for over twenty years, I've been paid to model professionally, and my photos have appeared in fitness magazines around the world.

I don't share that to brag or try to impress you, but simply to impress upon you that by making a disciplined commitment to anything in life will pay off with big rewards. It's worth it!

In order to become a successful entrepreneur in life with unlimited money, wealth, and prosperity is going to require you to make a disciplined commitment to your business until the day you die.

Besides being extremely wealthy, do you know what Bill Gates, Brad Pitt, Ellen DeGeneres, Oprah Winfrey, Ted Turner, Russell Simmons, Steve Jobs, John Mackey, Mark Zuckerberg, Tom Hanks, Lady Gaga, and Ralph Lauren all have in common? They dropped out of college so that they could make a disciplined commitment to following their dreams in life. The commitment they made all paid off.

Did you know that 99.75% of the world's population have thought about writing a book at some point in their lives, but less than 1% ever actually do? It's true. However, not only have I written twenty books, but I've become an International Best-Seller with books sold in fifteen different countries. I have decided to make a disciplined commitment to becoming a world-renowned coach, best-selling author and entrepreneur.

What are you passionate about? What do you love to do more than anything else? What are you willing to work harder at than anything else? What are you willing to make huge sacrifices for? If you're willing to make a disciplined commitment to your true passion in life, it will absolutely bring you an unlimited supply of money, wealth, and prosperity. Happiness too!

When you make a commitment to following your goals and dreams in life, you will never get bored or depressed. Making this commitment will bring out your true gifts and allow you to make a difference in people's lives all over the world. People will refer others to you and pay you huge amounts of money. You will be recognized and rewarded as being part of the most successful people in the world. I encourage you to make a disciplined commitment to whatever it is you think about the most. If you truly commit yourself to doing what you were born to do, it will give you satisfaction unlike anything else in the world. Your days will fly by and your work will be a blessing to others. Make a true commitment to your goals and dreams in life. I promise you, it will be worth it.

Chapter Nine:

Take Action!

The only way you're ever going to become a successful entrepreneur and have unlimited money, wealth, and prosperity is by taking massive action. Lazy people never achieve anything in life. The Holy Bible even says that being lazy will keep a person living in poverty:

How long will you lie there you sluggard? When will you get up from your sleep? A little sleep, a little slumber, a little folding of the hands to rest, and poverty will come on you like a thief and scarcity like an armed man. **Proverbs 6:9-11**

Entrepreneurs are not lazy people. It's impossible to be an entrepreneur if you're lazy. It just won't work out for you. Entrepreneurs are the hardest working people in the world. Please remember that entrepreneurs work over sixty hours per week, while the average employee only works forty hours per week. If employees could work less than forty hours per week and still have it count for full time, believe me, they most certainly would. There's a reason why employees are poor financially. It's their laziness. They don't ever go above and beyond. They do the bare minimum that they can get away with so that they won't get fired, but then wonder why their boss won't give them a raise. That makes me laugh!

One of my favorite quotes that I live by is: *How you do anything is how you do everything!* Entrepreneurship proves this true more than anything else. Employees and overweight people go hand in hand. The only way a person can become overweight is by being lazy. Lazy with their dietary habits and lazy with their work ethic. In my opinion, I will say that 99% of all employees will never become entrepreneurs because they're too lazy. They refuse to take action and work hard. Getting them to take action is like getting a new born baby to run a marathon. It's impossible!

Mark Zuckerberg of Facebook had an idea one day. The very second the idea came to him he immediately took massive action. He didn't wait. He didn't think about it. He didn't talk it over with his friends and family. He didn't weigh the pros with the cons. The only thing he did was take action immediately. That's the way every successful entrepreneur is.

If you want to become a successful entrepreneur you must do the same. This is non-negotiable. There isn't any way around this fact. Entrepreneurs are not lazy. We take action immediately. Once you know your reason "why" you must start taking action immediately.

When I wrote my first book, I had no idea what I was doing. I had never taken a writing class before. I didn't know any authors who could teach me how to properly format my book. I didn't know anyone who could edit my book for me. And, I most certainly didn't know how to market my book. However, I wrote, edited, published, and sold my very first copy in less than forty-eight hours. Within the first week, I had sold one hundred copies to people all over the country.

When my first shipment of books arrived at my home my wife and I were jumping up and down with excitement. Neither of us could believe that I was now a published author. We tore open the box to get a glimpse of the masterpiece that I had just released. As I opened the cover of the book my tongue fell out of my mouth and my heart sank to my stomach. There was no table of contents or page numbers. Oh my gosh! I wanted to cry. How in the world could I have forgot these two major components? My book had already sold over one hundred copies and not one of them had a table of contents or page numbers.

However, not one single person who had purchased my book had contacted me and told me there wasn't a table of contents or page numbers. They didn't even realize it. I did receive several testimonials from people telling me how much they appreciated me writing the book and sharing all of my weight loss secrets with them though. I had provided the reader with so much valuable content that they didn't even notice what was missing in the book. Most people in the world will never write or publish a book because they're waiting for some magical moment in time when everything is perfect. However, without knowing anything at all about publishing a book, I just decided to take massive action.

Not only was my book not perfectly written, but it didn't even contain a table of contents or page numbers. But, guess what? That book made me a published author, it has been bought or downloaded thousands of times, I have received tons of emails, requests, comments, and reviews, and it's even made me some money. The only difference between me and the other 99.75% of the people in the world who want to write a book is that I decided to take action. My wife and I will never forget that first book. We have the first copy of that book saved in our home as a piece of memorabilia. It's now a collector's item. That first book of mine without the table of contents and page numbers could someday be worth a lot of money to the few people who have a copy. So, if you happen to be one of those lucky people, hold onto that book. LOL.

My point in sharing that story with you is to demonstrate what taking action can do. Yes, you might screw up like I did, but not one single person even noticed my screw up except for me. However, because I decided to take action writing my first book, it made it possible for me to write my second, third, fourth, and every book since then.

Chapter Ten:

Don't Quit!

98% of the world's population are quitters. That's why very few people ever do anything great in life. Success is only for the few. Here's another one of my favorite quotes I'd like for you to remember: *Winners never quit and quitters never win.* If you want to become a successful entrepreneur and have an unlimited supply of money, wealth, and prosperity, you must never, ever quit.

My mom died when I was only nine years old. After she died my dad abused me until the day he kicked me out of his house when I was only fifteen years old. I've moved over one hundred times in my life. I've lived in nine states and I've been homeless in five of them. I've been in a car crash that could have killed me. I've lost every single penny I had on different business ventures at least five times. I've been lied to and cheated on by women who supposedly loved me more than anything. As close as I came to committing suicide, I didn't. When my wife and I decided to get married we didn't have a penny to our name. We didn't have wedding rings for the first year after we were married. My life has been hard. I lived in poverty for many years. I could have made up a thousand different excuses for myself to fail. I struggled in life, but I never quit.

When Jim Carrey was fourteen years old, his dad lost his job. His family hit some rough times. They moved into a Volks Wagon van on a relative's lawn and the young aspiring comedian started working eight hours per day after school to help his family.

When Jim was sixteen years old he dropped out of school to make a commitment to comedy full time. He moved to Los Angeles shortly after. He would park on Mulholland Drive every night and visualize himself becoming successful. On one of these nights he wrote himself a check for ten million dollars and made it out for: "Acting Services Rendered." He dated the check for Thanksgiving 1995. Just before that date, he landed the blockbuster role in the film *Dumb and Dumber*. He struggled in life, but he never quit!

Colonel Harland Sanders was fired from a variety of jobs throughout his career. In 1930, during the great depression, when he was forty years old, he started cooking chicken in his roadside Shell Service Station. He served people his chicken in his attached personal living quarters.

Over the next ten years, he perfected his secret recipe and pressure fryer cooking method for his famous fried chicken and moved onto bigger locations. His chicken was even praised in the media by famous food critic Duncan Hines. However, in the 1950's the interstate came through the Kentucky town where the Colonel's restaurant was located and it took away important road traffic. He was forced to close his business down. He was worried how he would survive off his meager $105 monthly pension check, so he set out to find restaurants who would franchise his secret recipe. He wanted a nickel for every piece of chicken that he sold. He drove around, slept in his car, and was rejected more than one thousand times before he found his first business partner. He struggled in life, but he never quit!

As a child, Oprah Winfrey was reportedly a victim of sexual abuse. She was repeatedly molested by her cousin, an uncle, and a family friend. She became pregnant and gave birth to a child when she was just fourteen years old. Her baby died just two weeks later. However, Oprah went on to finish high school as an honors student and earned a full scholarship to college. She worked her way up through the ranks of television. Today, she is a Billionaire! She struggled in life, but she never quit!

Every successful actor, model, writer, athlete, and business owner has struggled at some point throughout their lives, but what made them successful is that they never quit. Prepare yourself mentally for challenges to arise. If you'll simply get back up more times than you fall down, you will succeed.

Entrepreneurship is not easy, but nothing worth having is. If you've never stepped out on your own before, be prepared. As soon as you leave your normal, comfortable, nine to five, dead end job, the people closest to you will start telling you that you're crazy. They will do everything they can to talk you out of following your goals and dreams in life. If you go on to become a successful entrepreneur, you will make them feel inferior and insignificant. For this reason, they will try to keep you on their level.

Don't allow anyone to keep you from having an unlimited supply of money, wealth, and prosperity. There is nothing good, noble, or spiritual about being poor. Living a life of destitute poverty is a selfish way to live. The best thing you can do for the poor is not to be one of them.

Having an unlimited supply of money, wealth, and prosperity will not only help you sleep better at night, but it will also keep stress away and allow you to be a blessing to others. No one remembers someone who is poor, homeless, and insignificant in life. However, if you're a successful entrepreneur with unlimited money, wealth, and prosperity, you can give people jobs, feed the needy, clothe the naked, and donate to charities and less fortunate people all over the world. You can leave a legacy for your heirs that come after you.

Building a successful business will not be easy, but it will be worth it. If you're ready to start a business for less than $1,000 that has unlimited income potential and have me be your personal mentor, read on.

Chapter Eleven:
Dream Come True Business.

Since this is my book and I want to help you get rich, let me give you my personal advice. I truly practice what I preach. So, I'm only going to tell you to do something that I've already done and continue to do. I've owned many different types of businesses throughout my life, so here's some important things you want to look for in a potential business model.

Start a home-based business of some kind. This will allow you to work from home, work whenever you want, call your own shots, and spend a lot of time with your family.

Start a business that pays you residual income. Residual income is money that comes in long after the work has been finished. Without residual income, you'll have to work for the rest of your life.

Start a business that you can scale all over the world and that can impact millions of people's lives.

Find a successful mentor who has the experience to coach you.

It took me a whopping thirty years to find a business model that offered all four of these amazing benefits. That business is ACN.

By becoming a home-based business owner with ACN, you have all the following benefits available to you:

-Get to work from home.

-Get to earn residual income.

-Get to build a global business.

-Get to have a successful mentor.

Let me tell you why I think starting your own home-based business with ACN is the greatest business model you could ever start:

1. Very low start-up cost. At much less than $1,000 to start, you can make your money back and become profitable in less than a week.

2. No employees to deal with. ACN hires, trains, pays, and handles all the employees that work for you on the back end, so you can just focus on building your business.

3. Unlimited residual income potential. Unlike working at a job, with ACN there is no limit to how much money you can earn.

4. You can build a global company from the comfort of your own home. ACN is on four different continents and expanding every single year.

5. You can join my team and work with me. I will personally teach you everything you need to know for you to become successful.

6. You get to help people change their lives for a living. There's no better feeling than being able to help people around the world:
-fire their boss.
-get out of debt.
-become financially free.
-travel all over the world.
-spend more time with their family.

I have never seen a business model that offers so many positive benefits, yet has such a low start-up cost. ACN has truly changed my life in every area imaginable and I know it can do the same for you. Let me ask you a few brief questions:

-Do you ever watch tv?

-Do you have a cell phone?

-Do you ever use the internet?

-Do you use gas and/or electricity?

-Do you have any valuables in your home that are worth securing?

If you answered "yes" to any of these questions, then you're already a part of ACN. Don't you think you should make it official and start getting paid for doing the same things that I do? If you're confused, allow me to explain.

ACN is the world's largest provider of essential services that **YOU** and **EVERYONE YOU KNOW** already use every single day. Instead of paying these bills every month for the rest of your life, ACN allows you to get paid when people all over the world pay these bills every month for the rest of their lives. Which one sounds better to you: pay bills every single month, or get paid when people pay bills every single month? Exactly! It's a complete no brainer. If you're interested in learning more about how you can start getting paid residual income every single month for the rest of your life when people all over the world pay their monthly bills, simply watch the video on my website and then give me a call: www.ChangeYourLifeOvernight.com

If you enjoyed reading this book, here's more books by the author:

-Sell Your First Book

-Vision Board Success

-Faith Produces Miracles

-My Inspiring True Life Story

-Money Meditation Manifestation

-Network Marketing Success, Failure, & Everything In Between

-How To Lose Weight With Intermittent Fasting

Success: The Secret To Becoming Happy, Healthy, And Wealthy

-How To Make Money As An Author Selling Your Books On Amazon

All books can be purchased from:

www.amazon.com/author/fitchristophermitchell